JoJo

A Tiny Story of Faith

A Journey Through Adoption

Faith Miller

Illustrated by Joyce Knarr

Abingdon Press

JoJo, A Tiny Story of Faith
A Journey Through Adoption

ISBN 0-687-027608

Acknowledgements

Ruth Charles

Robin Campbell

David Lawrence

Susan Jacobs

Carol Baklarz

James Roland and the
  Sarasota *Herald-Tribune*

Joe Dicairano

Amy Tremblay

Lawson McKenzie

Dorothy and John Munneke

Roxanne Farmanfarmaian

Sondi Miller

Joe Popalaeo

Dennis Wilson

Cim Hirsch

David Stenglein

Patrick McDonough

Angela Harwell

Jean Luker

02 03 04 05 06 07 08 09 10 11 – 10 9 8 7 6 5 4 3 2 1

Printed in Hong Kong

To My Parents

Ida and Fountain Bowman

To Daddy,

From the moment you lifted me up into your arms,
I knew I would always be "daddy's little girl."

To Mom,

Only now can I understand how much you loved me.
You are now with the angels that brought us together … and I
will love you forever and always. This is our story, and this book
is my gift to you.

To Tina and Scott,

You are the miracles of my life. Your generous love and support has
shown me how really wonderful it is to be a mother. With all of my
heart and soul, I dedicate this family journey of faith to you.

Presented to

_____

From _____

Date _____

Once upon a time, not so very long ago, a beautiful baby girl was brought into the world. Now in itself the birth of a child is not all that remarkable, for babies are born every day. However, how this certain little girl came to be, and what transpired before her second birthday, was extraordinary. In fact, you will hardly believe that this is a true story, for it seems more like a fairy tale. But I promise you that if you will listen with your heart, the angels will whisper to you—*it was a miracle!*

This is the story of Sarah and Ethan, a special love story. It is a story that you must read carefully, for it is filled with both sublime happiness and unbearable woe! It is the tale of a young couple who may remind you of someone you have met before. They were soulfully devoted to one another, and had been in love since their early teens. Their marriage was filled with immeasurable joy … well, almost.

Sarah was lovely and rather petite, with a feisty spirit of joy and determination. She absolutely adored life and was never satisfied to sit by and wait for adventures to knock on her door. She lived each and every day to the fullest!

Ethan was a supremely handsome man, but it wasn't his dashing good looks that drew Sarah to him. Oh, no. It was his amazingly patient and generous spirit that set him apart from all the rest. He was as quiet and shy as Sarah was talkative and sociable, but his quiet demeanor gave only a hint of the soul lying within. Ethan was a good man, devoted both to Sarah and to God. That devotion was noticed by all the people who lived in the village. It was that very devotion that one day changed their lives forever!

From the earliest years of their marriage, Sarah and Ethan had longed for a child. But try as they might, nothing seemed to work. Ethan dearly loved Sarah, and he kept reassuring her that if they were patient, in due time their dream would be fulfilled.

Sarah dearly loved Ethan, but alas, one morning she arose and that was it! She was far too impatient to wait any longer! She desperately wanted a child and she truly believed, in the very depths of her soul, that there *must* be a secret—a special secret that she could uncover. She vowed to leave no stone unturned in her search for a child. She would become relentless in her journey to become a mother!

And so, in their sixth year of marriage, the couple set out on a journey to find an answer for dear, sweet Sarah. They traveled throughout the land asking stranger after stranger for advice. "How can we have children? What can we possibly do?" Sarah truly believed that an answer was just around the next corner.

ot long into their journey Sarah and Ethan came across a lively couple whose ten children raced through their home like untamed ponies. How is it that they were able to have so many children?

"We don't know!" the couple replied. "We just turn around and 'poof,' there they are! We can barely afford to feed and clothe them all! Boys and more boys! Girls and more girls! It's truly amazing! Our great love for children *must* be the secret!"

Sarah and Ethan were puzzled, for they too had a great love for children.

That wasn't the secret!

They journeyed on and sought out the most famous, most respected scientists in all the land.

"Please tell us what we might do in order to have children," Sarah pleaded.

The scientists cautiously prescribed very secret formulas, herbal remedies, and bubbling potions for them.

Sarah and Ethan studied and ate, studied and drank, ate and drank. They became very wise and very full, but they still didn't have a baby.

That wasn't the secret!

At last, months into their journey, when Ethan was very, very tired, and Sarah was very, very disappointed, they arrived at the golden gates of the Wisest Man in all the land. He welcomed them in with open arms. "I've been waiting for you," he said.

He led them through his beautiful exotic gardens, pausing by magnificent fountains, reflecting pools, and marble statues of children at play. It was breathtaking!

The Wise Man smiled warmly and reassured them that if they would listen carefully—if they would only listen with their hearts—he would reveal the secret they sought.

The Wise Man spoke carefully, choosing each thought and word as he related miraculous tales of faith, stories of heaven, of angels, and of miracles. Ethan and Sarah were spellbound by his tales of the power of prayer.

Following an afternoon filled with wondrous teachings, the Wise Man instructed the couple to return home and ponder his words. Promising them joy and happiness if they would heed his simple admonitions of faith and prayer, he bid them adieu, encouraging them to believe in miracles.

Sarah's soul was overwhelmed with gratitude, and Ethan's heart was no longer troubled. They had been deeply touched by their visit with the Wise Man. It was so clear, so very simple—prayerful hearts and an unwavering faith would most surely deliver their miracle, the child for whom they so desperately longed.

And so they prayed. And waited. And prayed. And waited.

In the early spring, soon after their return from their travels, Ethan set about to build a new cottage for Sarah, a new home with a strong foundation of invigorating faith and hope for the future! The cottage had lofty stone chimneys and thatched English dormers. Massive windows looked out on views of lavender and wildflowers. Theirs was now a home for a family, a home where their miracle child would soon frolic with her friends, ride her speckled pony, and swing from the tallest trees.

When the dust had cleared, when all the pictures were hung and the furniture was in place, the couple prepared a lavish storybook bedroom for their daughter. Ethan painstakingly carved a canopy bed from the sweetest pine trees in the forest, finishing it perfectly with a plush feather mattress worthy of a little princess!

Then it was Sarah's turn. Just like her mother before her, and her mother's mother before her, she began to decorate the child's room with treasures reminiscent of her own childhood wonder. Sarah draped the windows with yards and yards of flowing lace curtains. She set teeny-tiny teacups on a teeny-tiny table surrounded by teeny-tiny chairs. She lovingly placed teddy bears with soft, pudgy bellies on hand-quilted cushions.

Books filled with classic tales of fairies and princesses, paper dolls, and colorful balls lined the knotty pine bookshelves. Standing guard night and day, very tall, very serious wooden soldiers in magnificent gold and blue uniforms watched and waited for the miracle to arrive.

Perhaps the most beautiful sight in the sun-kissed room was Sarah's collection of porcelain dolls from all around the world. With wide eyes, heart-shaped lips, and colorful costumes, they lined the windowsills—perfectly positioned, vying for the first peek at the little girl who was coming to make them her own.

Sarah and Ethan prayed. And waited. And prayed. And waited.

And the seasons passed slowly by, one long day, one long week, one long month at a time. Winter melted into spring. Summer was swept away by the blustery winds of fall.

In the ninth year of their marriage, when winter returned, the sky turned unusually gloomy and gray. The air became unbearably frigid. Gigantic gusts of snow whipped through the valley, swirling into peaks of white marshmallow frosting, blanketing the frail fields of lavender and wildflowers. The windowpanes of the storybook bedroom rattled, and long crystal icicles dripped from the dormers.

Along with the heavy blanket of snow, an even heavier blanket of sadness enveloped Sarah, Ethan, and their beautiful home. There was no pitter-patter of tiny footsteps in the hallways, no music or laughter from the very cold, very silent storybook bedroom. The teddy bears huddled together in the corners. The teacups sat empty and the porcelain dolls shivered, while the brave toy soldiers stood still watching, patiently waiting for the little girl. Where was she?

Unbearable loneliness darkened their lives. Their sadness was so great that even the fires Ethan built in their fireplaces could not warm their hearts.

The child they had waited and prayed for had not come. Perhaps their prayers had not reached heaven. But that could not be! The Wise Man had taught them that all prayers are heard in heaven.

Sarah wept. Ethan began to doubt his faith. He blamed himself. *This must be my fault. I have failed Sarah. Perhaps my faith is not strong enough.*

Not a word was spoken aloud. The crackling of the fires and the moaning of the wind were the only sounds in the forlorn, frozen cottage. The lonely couple could not even comfort each other. Their sorrow was too much to bear.

They no longer prayed. They no longer waited. They lost all hope.

In the late afternoon of the very coldest, the very saddest of all days, when he was quite certain that all hope was lost, Ethan whispered, "I'm so sorry," to his dear wife. He bundled up in his warmest woolen overcoat and gray flannel hat and headed out into the frigid wind and snow. Sarah watched tearfully as he slowly disappeared down the snow-covered cobblestone path.

With his head hung oh-so-low and his footsteps oh-so-slow, Ethan began his lonely journey. He needed this time to gather his thoughts, talk to God, and seek understanding for his broken heart.

Are you there? Do you hear me? Do you feel my pain? I am your faithful son, Ethan. Have I not been prayerful enough? Have I not shown enough patience? Are you testing my devotion? Have I ever given you a reason to doubt my love for Sarah?

If there is any reason at all why my prayers have not been answered, what is it? I built our home with my own hands to prepare for our child.

Should I give up hope, disregard your teaching after all this time? I just don't understand! Heavenly Father, I beg of you, do not forsake me! Give me the courage to go on and the strength to comfort Sarah. Please! Show me the way!

Lost in his prayers and lost in time, blinded by confusion and the snowstorm surrounding him, Ethan trudged on—mile upon mile to nowhere. And when the bitter chill became intolerable, he sought refuge in the warmth of the village marketplace, hurrying into a familiar, cozy, corner grocery store.

As he stomped his boots to shake off the snow, Ethan caught his sad reflection in the frozen panes of the store window.

Drying his eyes with the back of his now stiff, frozen gloves, he regained his composure. He began to slowly fill his basket with odds and ends that he didn't even need. In his overwhelming state of despair, he wandered aimlessly up and down the aisles, paying little attention to his surroundings.

He walked right by a young woman at least two times before he even noticed her. She was pushing a tiny baby girl in a rickety wooden stroller. As he passed them by for the third time, he could hear the little girl singing softly to her rag doll—a doll with the saddest blue eyes, a tear on its cheek, and a face as soiled as her own. "JoJo, my JoJo," she sang over and over as she hugged the doll to her heart. Ethan paused and caught himself staring at the poor young woman. He watched as she carefully counted her coins before placing one small jug of milk and one box of cereal into the stroller with her child.

Her tattered cotton coat was unbuttoned, revealing a thin, frail body. Her long brown hair was matted and damp from the melting snowflakes. Her cheeks were flushed from the winter wind; and despite her obvious poverty and the cold, she was actually beautiful.

Ethan noticed that she spoke to her child in a weak whisper. Was she ill? The young woman glanced over at Ethan. He was embarrassed for staring and quickly looked away. Too late! Her deep brown eyes caught his stare, and when he looked back, her eyes were fixed on him. *Why is she looking at me? Why am I so drawn to her? How curious!* he thought. And then as he turned to walk away, she approached him.

"Excuse me, can you please help me?" Kaitlin slowly began. "Can you possibly help me with my baby? I'm all alone and I've been so very ill. I have so little money…"

Tears began to fill her large brown eyes. She prayed to heaven for help. *Oh, heavenly Father, please. Help me touch his heart! I need you now, more than ever before. I can't do this alone. Where shall I begin? Where shall I start?*

Kaitlin had had a most joyful childhood, growing up embraced by loving parents who instilled in her an unwavering faith. They taught her to pray when she was a very little girl. She would kneel by her father's side every night and recite, "Now I lay me down to sleep...."

Her prayers were for happiness, love, and laughter. And indeed her world was filled with beautiful things.

Kaitlin and her friends adored playing dress-up, pretending that one day their handsome princes would appear on marvelous white stallions and whisk them away to beautiful castles where they would live happily ever after.

"Hooray! Hooray!" they would shout, and fall to the ground in laughter!

In the spring of her seventeenth year, in one exceptionally beautiful moment in time, her handsome prince arrived. He swept into her life, fulfilling all her dreams.

Jonathan was tall and blond, with the bluest eyes she had ever seen. With his dashing smile and commanding presence, he instantly won her heart. On the day of their wedding, the whole village rejoiced and a great celebration was held to honor the happy couple! The fairy tale had come true! The Princess had found her charming Prince!

Life was exactly as she had prayed it would be—joyful and beautiful. And in due time, with the blessed birth of a beautiful daughter and a strong, loving husband by her side, Kaitlin's life became absolutely perfect! She gave thanks to heaven and the angels who watched over her.

As their daughter's first birthday approached, Kaitlin sketched a pattern for a rag doll for her precious baby to play with. In fact, she drew the pattern to look just like Jonathan. Night after night she curled up by the fire and carefully hand-stitched the little doll. Stitch by stitch, loop by loop, she lovingly recreated Jonathan's blue eyes. His smile was there, too, along with yellow yarn for the hair. Jonathan provided black flannel from the lining of his hunting jacket for the little boots. Kaitlin used scraps of red calico and the bluest of cotton for the doll's tiny shirt and pants.

When the last stitch was tied and the rag doll was perfect, they wrapped a big, red ribbon around their gift and gave it to their daughter.

The child's eyes grew large with excitement as she hugged the doll to her heart and babbled, "JoJo. My JoJo."

From that moment on, the baby and JoJo were inseparable.

Kaitlin's heart was full to overflowing with love for her little family.

But now, less than a year later, heart-wrenching sadness had replaced Kaitlin's joy. Her beloved parents had both gone to heaven and Jonathan was gone as well, killed in a war that had swept across their country. Kaitlin had been left in the mere springtime of her life, penniless, devastated, and alone to raise her precious daughter.

The excruciating sadness left her ill in body and spirit. She could not bear to go on without Jonathan! She could neither eat nor drink. Kaitlin's broken heart was too much for her to bear. Each time she looked at JoJo, the little rag doll, she was reminded of the sweet nights by the fire when Jonathan had helped her fashion the tiny flannel boots. The doll became a daily reminder of a happier time, a time of wonder and enchantment. She knew that Jonathan had loved her and their child and she vowed never to forget that love; but that time had passed and now she had to find the best path to care for her daughter.

Kaitlin cried out from the depths of her soul, "What is to become of me? What will I do? How can I go on?"

She prayed unceasingly every morning and every night. But she no longer prayed for herself, she prayed only for her baby daughter—for *her* protection, for *her* destiny, for *her* happiness.

With her baby by her side, she bowed her head and prayed. Her prayers as a mother were not so different from those of her childhood. "Now I lay me down to sleep … dear Lord, please help me find a way to provide for my precious baby. I am so ill, so weak, so lost! Show me the way. Lead me to the path I must take. Give me the courage to do what is best … And if I should die before I wake.…"

Then late one afternoon, a most peculiar thing happened. It was an especially dark and dreary day; in fact, the very coldest, most frozen day of the year. As she was preparing the baby's dinner, the last bottle of milk curiously rolled off the counter and shattered on the cold cottage floor.

Reluctantly, Kaitlin was forced to bundle up her baby, slip into her thin cotton coat, and venture out into the frigid ice and snow. With her head held oh-so-low and her footsteps oh-so-slow, Kaitlin, her baby, and the rag doll named JoJo began their journey to the village marketplace.

Loving angels followed along. They knew exactly what was about to take place.

Startled by Kaitlin's approach, Ethan listened in awe as she continued to speak.

"Please. Would you consider caring for my baby? She is such a blessing. Her father and I have loved her more than life itself." Kaitlin paused as Ethan stepped back away from her.

"Why, my dear child, you can't possibly be serious! How can I care for your baby? You do not even know me. I am a complete stranger to you. Have you no family? Have you no friends?" Ethan scolded.

He was shocked that the young woman would even suggest such a thing! He and Sarah had prayed for a child for almost ten years. And here *she* was, blessed with a beautiful daughter and yet pleading with a stranger to take her! For shame! For shame!

Kaitlin hung her head. She was so humiliated, so ashamed. Did this stranger see her as a beggar? This was not how she had expected him to react! She wanted desperately to turn and run away, but her legs wouldn't move. She closed her eyes and returned to the sweet memories of happily ever after. How cruel fate had been. She must make Ethan understand. If he could only see her as she was!

The angels encircling her whispered, "Be strong, Kaitlin. Go on. We're right here with you."

She opened her eyes and saw right through to Ethan's heart, to his very spirit! Summoning all her courage (and with help from above), she continued to plead, "Please don't walk away! You are no stranger to me, Ethan. I know all about you and your lovely wife, Sarah. I have heard the amazing stories about your travels far and wide, and your search for a child of your own. Many in the village have seen your beautiful home with the porcelain dolls and brave toy soldiers!"

"WHAT? What have you heard?" Ethan sharply replied. "What do you know about me … about us? Do you know that our hearts are broken? Can you feel our pain? You could never begin to comprehend how lost and forlorn we feel. Do you know that as you hold your child tonight, we have nothing left to hold to? We have finally lost all hope. Our prayers have never been answered!"

Ethan's voice trembled with anguish. His face was numb to the tears that rolled down his cheeks. *Who does this woman think she is? Why doesn't she just go away and leave me alone?*

Kaitlin reached out and gently touched his arm. "Don't you realize that, like you, others have lost hope? You are not the first couple to be in despair, Ethan. But now *I know!* I know why the milk rolled off the counter and why I met you in *this* store *tonight*. I know! Don't you see? God did hear my prayers, and oh, Ethan, God heard yours also. We were meant to be here. My baby is the baby you have prayed for, and you and Sarah are the answer to my prayers and dreams. It all makes so much sense! Can't you see? Please, Ethan! My baby needs you. Don't turn away from her!"

Could it be that this young woman loved her child so much that she would be willing to part with her in order to give her a better life? Was it possible that a mother could have such compassion? Did she really understand what she was asking him to do? If he and Sarah adopted this child, she would be theirs for all eternity!

Ethan shook his head in disbelief. His knees went weak. His heart was pounding. *Lord, is this young woman right? Have you brought me to such an unlikely place to answer my prayers? Is such a miracle possible?*

The baby's brown eyes pierced his heart. Her cherub face was delicately framed by fine, golden ringlets of hair peeking out from under the edges of her woolen bonnet. In the tiniest voice, she began to once again sing to her little rag doll, "JoJo, my JoJo. Love you, my JoJo."

And then, as if by some predetermined destiny, some miracle of fate, the baby girl reached up and touched him! She clutched his fingers in her tiny hands and offered her doll to him.

Ethan melted! He wished that Sarah were there, that she could see what happened! It was Sarah who always displayed such great faith, such compassion! It was Sarah who believed in miracles! Surely she would understand that with that simple touch of a baby's hand, his life had been changed forever! Ethan looked at the young mother, took a long, deep breath, and mustering all of his courage, said, "All right. All right. I will help you. I will help you."

Kaitlin clasped her hands to her heart and exclaimed, "Bless you! Oh bless you, Ethan! God has answered my prayers. Bless you! Bless you!"

She continued. "Please make me one promise. Will you see to it that she keeps her rag doll? Perhaps as she holds it to her heart each day, she will somehow remember that I made it for her and that it looks like her father who loved her very much. But now she is your daughter. From now on you are her father."

"Her father!" Ethan could hardly believe his ears. "Her father!"

Kaitlin went on, "When you feel the time is right, Ethan, please tell her how much her father and I loved her."

And then as the reality of the moment set in, Kaitlin reached down and lifted her daughter out of the stroller for the last time. Kneeling in front of her baby, her fingers trembling, Kaitlin bravely fastened the little buttons on her daughter's coat, smoothed her golden locks, and straightened her bonnet. The baby's brown eyes sparkled as she turned and proudly smiled at Ethan, all the while continuing to hug her rag doll as she rocked back and forth.

Quite unexpectedly, she began to dance in the aisle with JoJo. Kaitlin joined her, taking the baby's little hands in her own, all the while softly singing a familiar children's song,

> *Ring around the rosies. Pocket full of posies.*
> *Ashes. Ashes. We all fall down.*

For a brief moment all was well with the world. All was beautiful once more—mother and daughter in perfect rhythm, in perfect time.

This was the most dreadful, the most tragic moment Ethan had ever witnessed. He kept telling himself, *It's going to be all right. It's going to be all right. This is best for the baby! Sarah and I will love her as our own! Heaven has performed this miracle. It's going to be all right!*

The innocent child looked from her mother to Ethan and from Ethan back to her mother. She climbed into her mother's lap, kissing Kaitlin's face over and over and wiping away Kaitlin's tears with her little hands. "Mommy. My mommy. Love you, Mommy," she whimpered.

She was too little, too young to understand why her mother and this big, strong man were so sad. She had no idea that her world was about to change!

Kaitlin kissed her daughter once, twice, three times!

She hugged her tighter than she ever had before. Over and over she whispered, "Forgive me. Forgive me, my precious, precious baby. I will love you forever and ever! For always and ever more."

Slowly, very, very slowly (it must have seemed like an eternity), Kaitlin rose, blotted her tears with a delicate handkerchief, and softly whispered, "It's time. It's time. We must do this for our baby, Ethan."

In the village square, the chimes in the steeple announced the new hour … clang, clang, clang, clang, clang, clang, clang. And with a mother's heartbeat, time stood still. The earth paused in great reverence. The moon hid its face behind the clouds, and Kaitlin handed her baby to her new father.

Ethan trembled as he reached out his arms for the baby girl. She stared deep into his eyes, tilted her head, and lovingly held out her doll for him. It was as if she had known Ethan forever! When he lifted her up to his chest, she hugged his neck and her rag doll accidently slipped out and fell to the floor.

Carefully balancing the child and his basket, he bent down to pick up the doll. When he stood up and turned around to speak to Kaitlin, she was gone. He turned round and round, but she had vanished!

Utterly bewildered, Ethan rushed into the street, following her footsteps in the snow until they mysteriously disappeared from view.

Pushing his way through the passersby, he ran to and fro calling, desperately searching for the young mother! Where had she gone? He had so much to ask her! What was her name? What was her baby's name? He had so many questions! Where had she gone?

The evening shadows and the blinding snowfall made it impossible to find her. At last he accepted that she was gone. Looking down at the face of the child nestled in his arms, he felt a kind of peace slip over him. The pleas of a young woman and the prayers of a lonely couple had been answered at last. On the most unlikely night, in the most unlikely of places, the angels of heaven had joined two very special families together. *It was truly a miracle!*

Carrying his new daughter, Ethan had walked only a couple of blocks when he caught a glimpse of a beautiful little red velvet coat with white fur trim and matching bonnet displayed in the window of the children's shop across the street.

He knew instantly what he must do!

"My dearest child," Ethan beamed, "let's surprise Sarah!"

He burst through the wooden doors of the shop, clanging the large brass bell for immediate attention! Astonished by his exuberance but thrilled to share in the moment, the salesladies agreed to fulfill Ethan's request. They gently took the little girl and her rag doll by the hand and disappeared into the back of the shop.

When the salesladies returned with his baby, his little angel, this child from heaven, Ethan fell to his knees and gave thanks from the deepest depths of his soul! Here, standing before him, clad in the beautiful red velvet coat with white fur trim and matching bonnet, was his new daughter.

The women beamed with pride as the little girl ran to her new father. When she held out JoJo for him to kiss, her big brown eyes sparkled. Ethan could hardly believe his eyes—she looked so much like the porcelain dolls that were waiting for her at home. He whisked her up in his arms and they hurried across town, home to his lovely wife and the baby's new mother!

When they finally arrived at the cottage, Ethan burst through the front door and shouted, "Sarah! Sarah! Come quickly! Come and see what I found at the market!"

Sarah hurried down the steps and stared in utter disbelief at her husband and the baby girl in his arms! Aghast, she cried, "Ethan, what are you doing? Whose baby is this? Have you lost your senses?"

She stood there, absolutely speechless, as Ethan proceeded to tell her the story of the young mother and her pleas for compassion. "How can this be?" she wondered.

"Ethan, where is this young woman? Who was she? How did she hear about us?"

"Sarah, can't you see?" Ethan was exasperated. "I don't know who she was or how she heard about us, but she knew, Sarah. She knew all about our prayers and our years of waiting. She said that she had been praying, too. She said that heaven brought us together.

"Perhaps she was an angel herself. I just don't know, Sarah. But can't you see? This is the miracle that we've been waiting for—the miracle we've been praying for! I'm so ashamed that we lost hope. God did hear us, Sarah, and now God has delivered this beautiful child for us to raise as our own. It's a miracle."

Sarah hesitated, then walked over, somewhat shyly, to Ethan and the baby girl. When the baby saw her coming, she held out her arms and offered her doll to Sarah. "JoJo. My JoJo," she said proudly.

Sarah knelt down by her side and answered, "Yes, sweetheart. This is your JoJo. Would you like to see your new bedroom? It's full of beautiful dolls, teacups, and teddy bears. They've all been waiting a very, very long time for you!"

As the new mother and her child walked together, hand-in-hand for the very first time, Sarah paused and smiled back at her husband. "Ethan, I think we should name our new daughter Faith, for it was surely because of our faith and the unbelievable courage of her mother that we have all been brought together. Oh, Ethan, the Wise Man was right! Our miracle was granted! The darling angel we have longed for has been delivered at last!"

Many years later the baby girl named Faith grew into a beautiful woman and was blessed with a son and a daughter of her own. She cannot remember that snowy evening or the salesladies who dressed her in red velvet, but JoJo still sits on her bed to remind her of the tale that her parents told her years before they passed away.

Faith explains to her children why her father always called her his "little angel" and how he swore that the dimples in her cheeks were where the angels had kissed her! She loves to tell her children why her parents named her Faith, and how thankful she is for the amazing power of prayer in their lives!

And each time her daughter wants to know more about the young woman who gave her life, Faith hugs her very old, very tattered JoJo, and shares the story one more time.

"That young woman, my mother, brought me to your Grandpa Ethan and your Grandmother Sarah at a very special moment in time—when they had lost all hope and were ready to abandon their prayers. I truly believe it was all meant to be.

"God never forgets us. Remember, sweetheart, no matter how long it takes, or what the circumstances of our lives, we must never stop praying. Our prayers will always be answered in due time—that is what faith is all about."